Dessert Recipes Book: Delicious and Healthy Recipes

ASAN SORINA

CONTENS
Dessert Recipes Book: Delicious and Healthy Recipes

Chocolate brownie and mascarpone

The simplest brownie recipe. It is made from only two ingredients

Traditional Easter with dough, sweet cheese and raisins

Glazed check with lemon and poppy seeds

Sticky blackberry with chocolate

Magic cheesecake

Kinder Pingui cake

Shadow chocolate cake (in gradients)

Basbousa semolina cake

Cake with sheets and chocolate cream

Snow White cake with coconut cream

Christmas cake with dried fruits and nuts

Homemade cake with cottage cheese and apricots

Peach Cobbler – Peach Cobbler

Cake with strawberries and mascarpone cream

Strawberry cheesecake

Cheesecake with Nutella and strawberries

Cabana Cake (Roofing)

Cherry cheesecake

Pineapple cheesecake

Cheesecake with Oreo cookies without oven

"Danube Waves" cake with cherries and chocolate

Cream Cream – Cream with vanilla cream

Measurement

standards

COMMON COOKING EQUIVALENCES

1 PINCH	⟷	1/8 TSP
1 DRY OUNCE	⟷	1/16 POUND
1 POUND	⟷	16 OUNCES
1 TEASPOON	⟷	1/3 TABLESPOON
1 TABLESPOON	⟷	3 TEASPOONS
1 FLUID OUNCE	⟷	1/8 CUP
1/4 CUP	⟷	4 TABLESPOONS
1 CUP	⟷	8 FLUID OUNCES
1 PINT	⟷	2 CUPS
1 QUART	⟷	2 PINTS
1 GALLON	⟷	4 QUARTS

PALEO BLACKBERRIES WITHOUT FLOUR AND WITHOUT SUGAR

INGREDIENTS

1/2 cup coconut powder

1/2 cup cocoa or carob powder

1/2 cup coconut butter

3 eggs

1/2 cup natural bee honey

grated peel of a lemon

50 g hazelnuts or walnuts for decoration

METHOD OF PREPARATION

Learn how to make delicious blackberries, according to a paleo recipe, without flour and without sugar, perfect for the little ones.

Method of preparation:

Preheat the oven to 150 degrees and grease a yena bowl or higher pan with butter or oil.

Mix all ingredients carefully, either manually or in a blender or food processor.

Pour the paleo black dough and bake for about 30 minutes, until the toothpick inserted in the middle of the cake comes out clean.

Leave to cool for about 30 minutes before cutting and serving.

Keep away from air, keep fresh for a few days at room temperature or in the refrigerator.

Good appetite!

Black woman with mascarpone and white chocolate

If you are a black fan, you must try this delicious black recipe with mascarpone and white chocolate. It's a delight. It can be garnished with fruit, nuts or melted chocolate.

150 g dark chocolate
4 eggs
150 g butter
100 g powdered sugar
70 g of flour
100 g white chocolate
150 g mascarpone
walnut, fruit, cocoa or melted chocolate for serving

METHOD OF PREPARATION:

The dark chocolate is broken into squares and the butter is cut into cubes. Put in a saucepan and melt in a bain-marie and stir slowly. After the composition has become homogeneous, add sugar and three eggs, one at a time and stir constantly. After everything becomes homogeneous, add flour. The obtained composition is poured into a form greased with butter and leveled, then set aside to prepare white chocolate with mascarpone.

Put the broken white chocolate in a saucepan and melt it in a bain-marie. After it has melted, add the mascarpone cream and an egg and mix well. The obtained composition is poured into the tray over the dark chocolate and baked for only 25 minutes. Then remove from the oven and leave for another 10 minutes in the pan.

The obtained blackberry is then removed, allowed to cool, and then garnished with walnuts, cocoa, fruit or melted chocolate.

Good appetite!

Cheesecake with apricots

Cheesecake with apricots. I tell you it's so fluffy and tasty that every mouthful melts in your mouth.

FOR Dough
- 300 g flour
- 150 g butter
- 3 tablespoons sugar
- 80 ml milk or lukewarm water
- a pinch of salt

FOR FILLING
- 1 kg of cottage cheese
- 3 tablespoons semolina
- 6 eggs
- 200 g powdered sugar
- 10 apricots

METHOD OF PREPARATION:

We prepare the dough first. Put the flour in a bowl and mix with the salt, then add the soft butter and cut into cubes. Mix with your fingertips and, when it has become a sandy mixture, pour the milk or water. Stir and spread a sheet covering the bottom and walls of a baking tray.

For the filling, mix the cheese with the eggs, semolina and sugar. Place a layer of apricots on top of the dough, cleaned of the seeds and then the cheese.

Put the tray in the oven for 40 minutes.

Good appetite!

Sponge cake with raspberries

It's easy and fast and everyone likes it. Pandispan with raspberries is a fluffy and tasty dessert is suitable for any season. But, as summer is the fruit season, you can try it in different combinations, but my favorite is the one with raspberries.

INGREDIENTS

8 eggs
4 tablespoons oil
250 g sugar
a pinch of salt
250 g flour
300–400 g of raspberries
powdered sugar for serving

METHOD OF PREPARATION:

The egg whites are mixed with a pinch of salt and, when the foam starts to form, the sugar is poured.

Continue mixing for about 10 minutes, until a firm foam is obtained.

Add the yolks, one by one, mix, pour the oil, then add the flour and mix gently with a whisk.

Pour the dough into a cake pan, lined with baking paper, place the raspberries on top, and bake for 25–30 minutes. After cooling, cut and serve with powdered sugar on top.

Good appetite!

Quick raspberry pie

Quick raspberry pie. I really like raspberries. Today I went to the market and bought a kilogram. After I ate my fill, I quickly made this quick pie.

FOR DOUGH:
 350 g flour a tablespoon of sugar
 half a teaspoon of salt
 230 butter just taken out of the fridge and cut into cubes
 6 tablespoons very very cold water, possibly with a few ice cubes in it
 an egg yolk and a tablespoon of milk for greasing

FOR FILLING:
 600 g raspberries
 5 tablespoons sugar

2 tablespoons tapioca flour or cornstarch
 a tablespoon of lemon juice

METHOD OF PREPARATION:

How to prepare dough
1.Mix the flour with the butter until it looks like crumbs. Then add water and stir until the dough begins to bind. Be careful not to overdo the mixture because it will lose its tenderness.

2. Then divide into two balls, wrap the halves in cling film and refrigerate for an hour.

How to prepare the filling
Put the 600 grams of raspberries in a bowl, mix with 5 tablespoons of sugar and 2 tablespoons of tapioca flour or cornstarch and a tablespoon of lemon juice.

assembling
Preheat the oven to 200 degrees and remove one of the two dough balls from the refrigerator. Roll out half of the dough – it's good to work with the dough as quickly as possible, when it's cold it's more obedient and doesn't break very easily.
Place the dough in a tart pan lined with baking paper and greased with butter and cut the edges that fall over the tray, leaving only an edge of about 2 cm.

Pour the fruit into the pan and cover with the other spread sheet. This time do not cut the edges and try to "edge" them under the edge of the bottom dough, keeping your index finger under the dough and pressing, on both sides, with the index finger and thumb of the other hand. If you find it too complicated, you can cut the dough into strips and form a grid over the fruit (that's what I did). Before putting it in the oven, grease it with beaten egg yolk with a spoonful of milk, sprinkle caster sugar on top and increase it in a few places to get the air out (if you put a lid on).

Keep in the oven for an hour, until browned, and then leave to cool for at least an hour. Have it served as such, decorated with fruit or next to a cup of ice cream.

Good appetite!

Marquise cake with chocolate and cherries

Awning cake with chocolate and cherries is a delicacy ready in just 45 minutes.

MARCHISE INGREDIENTS WITH CHERRY AND CHOCOLATE
300 g of dark chocolate, put on a large grater or cut into small pieces
125 g unsalted butter, cut into cubes
1 teaspoon vanilla essence
6 yolks
165 g caster sugar
500 ml liquid cream
50 g cocoa, sifted

FOR FILLING CREAM:

400 g cherries in alcohol (from cherries)

FOR GLAZING:

100 g dark chocolate, chopped

A hand thawed cherries

METHOD OF PREPARATION:

In a non-stick pan over low heat, melt the chocolate, butter, vanilla. Stir to blend and set aside to cool.

Using a blender, combine the yolks with the sugar until you get a thick cream. Slow down and incorporate the chocolate mixture. Stir in the cocoa and then the cream. Be careful with the mixture, because it should not be too viscous, but easily spreadable.

Pour half of the amount into a cake tin, lined with greased baking paper, and place a layer of cherries in the center. Pour over the remaining composition and level the surface. Refrigerate and leave overnight. Transfer to the serving platter and refrigerate for at least 20 minutes.

For the icing, melt the chocolate in the microwave for a few minutes and let it cool. Sprinkle the awning and garnish with fresh thawed cherries. Let it cool for at least another hour before serving.

Good appetite!

Banana Bread with cherries

Banana Bread with cherries. It is made extremely quickly and is very tasty, children will not get tired of it. Grind the bananas, mix the ingredients and the goodness is ready.

INGREDIENTS
2–3 large bananas, well ripened

55 g butter, at room temperature

70 g Greek yogurt

160 g of brown sugar

1 or

1 teaspoon vanilla flavor

1 cup flour

1 teaspoon baking soda

½ teaspoon of baking powder
½ teaspoon of salt
1 cup pitted cherries, cut in half
2 tablespoons flour
160 g of chocolate pieces

METHOD OF PREPARATION:

1. Preheat the oven to 180 degrees and prepare a cake pan, lined with baking paper.

2. Peel the bananas, put them in a bowl and crush them with a fork. Then add over the egg, butter, Greek yogurt, brown sugar and vanilla and mix well until the composition is homogeneous.
3. In another bowl, mix the flour with the salt, baking soda and baking powder. Then add over the banana composition and mix a little. Add the chocolate pieces.

4. The cherries, peeled and cut in half, are given through the two tablespoons of flour, then added to the composition.

5. Pour the composition in the form lined with baking paper and leave in the oven for 65–70 minutes until it passes the toothpick test.

6. After removing it from the oven, leave it in the pan for another 10 minutes.

Good appetite!

Banana Bread with chocolate flakes

I don't like complicated desserts, but banana bread with chocolate is practically made on its own. Crush the bananas, mix the ingredients, put them in the pan and quickly put them in the oven. It doesn't take you more than 10 minutes to prepare it, and the taste is dreamy.

INGREDIENTS
3 ripe bananas
75 g of melted butter
100 g of sugar
1 egg, beaten well
1 teaspoon vanilla flavor
1 teaspoon baking powder
A pinch of salt

185 g of flour
 85 g of chocolate pieces

METHOD OF PREPARATION:

Preheat the oven to 180 degrees Celsius. Grease a cake pan with butter and line it with flour.

Put the three bananas in a bowl and crush them with a fork and mix well. Add the melted butter and mix until smooth. Add sugar, beaten egg, vanilla flavor, baking powder, salt, flour and mix well. Add the chocolate pieces and mix well from the bottom up. Pour the composition into the lined tray and place the chocolate pieces on top.

Leave in the oven for 50–60 minutes or until the toothpick test passes.

After removing from the oven, leave to cool and then serve

Good appetite!

American pie with cherries - the original recipe

American pie, a cake made of tender dough with butter full of aromatic fruit. Here is the original recipe. The taste is insane.

DOUGH INGREDIENT:
350 g flour
a spoon of sugar
half a teaspoon of salt
230 butter just taken out of the fridge and cut into cubes
6 tablespoons very very cold water, possibly with a few ice cubes in it
an egg yolk and a tablespoon of milk to grease
caster sugar for garnish

FILLING INGREDIENTS:

750 g fresh or frozen cherries

5 tablespoons sugar

2 tablespoons tapioca flour or cornstarch

a tablespoon of lemon juice

METHOD OF PREPARATION:

How to prepare dough

1.Mix the flour with the butter until it looks like crumbs. Then add water and stir until the dough begins to bind. Be careful not to overdo the mixture because it will lose its tenderness.

2. Then divide into two balls, wrap the halves in cling film and refrigerate for an hour.

How to prepare the filling

Put the 750 grams of fruit in a bowl, mix with 5 tablespoons of sugar and 2 tablespoons of tapioca flour or cornstarch and a tablespoon of lemon juice.

assembling

1. Preheat the oven to 200 degrees and remove one of the two dough balls from the refrigerator. Roll out half of the dough – it's good to work with the dough as quickly as possible, when it's cold it's more obedient and doesn't break very easily.

2.Place the dough in a tart pan lined with baking paper and greased with butter and cut the edges that fall over the tray, leaving only a margin of about 2 cm.

3. Pour the fruit into the pan and cover with the other spread sheet. This time do not cut the edges and try to "edge" them under the edge of the bottom dough, holding your index finger under the dough and pressing, on both sides, with the index finger and thumb of the other hand. If you find it too complicated, you can cut the dough into strips and form a grid over the fruit.

4. Before putting it in the oven, grease it with beaten egg yolk with a spoonful of milk, sprinkle caster sugar on top and increase it in a few places to get the air out.

5. Keep in the oven for an hour, until browned, and then leave to cool for at least an hour.

Good appetite!

Cake with vanilla cream and ness

WHEAT INGREDIENT

5 large eggs

7 tablespoons sugar

7 tablespoons oil

7 tablespoons flour

5 gr baking powder

VANILLA CREAM INGREDIENTS

500 ml of milk

half a cup of sugar

3 yolks

150 gr of butter

5 tablespoons flour

vanilla essence

NESS FOAM INGREDIENTS
3 egg whites
7 tablespoons sugar
3 ness sachets

METHOD OF PREPARATION:
countertop
Separate the eggs and beat the egg whites. Add the sugar in the rain and continue mixing until it melts.

The yolks are rubbed with baking powder (unquenched) and we start to gradually add the oil. Put a tablespoon of oil, then mix well, add another tablespoon, and mix and repeat until you put all 7 tablespoons of oil.

Pour this composition over the beaten egg whites. Add the flour and mix with a spoon from top to bottom, very lightly. Put the composition in a lined tray and put it in the oven until it passes the toothpick test. After baking, remove the top from the oven, leave to cool and cut in half lengthwise.

Vanilla cream
Mix the yolks with the sugar, add the flour, then the milk and incorporate.
Put on the fire and leave until it thickens. When it starts to thicken, turn it on low and stir constantly. When it has thickened enough, remove from the heat, add the soft butter and the essence, mix well and leave to cool.

Ness foam

Whisk the egg whites, add only 4 tablespoons of sugar in the rain and continue beating until melted. Add the 3 sachets of ness and mix well.

Separately, in a saucepan burn 3 tablespoons of sugar until it takes on a beautiful color. When the sugar has melted, pour it over the ness foam. Pour the burnt sugar with one hand and mix quickly with the other so that the sugar does not caramelize in the foam.

After the ness foam is ready, we start assembling the cake. Place the first top, over which the vanilla cream is spread, then place the second top over which the ness foam is spread. Garnish with grated chocolate and leave for a few hours, preferably overnight.

Good appetite!

Nutella cake

Do you like Nutella? Then you will love this simple and delicious Nutella cake, which is ready in just 15 minutes.

CRUST INGREDIENTS
175g of crushed chocolate chip cookies
85 g of melted butter
a pinch of salt

NUTELLA CAKE CREAM INGREDIENTS
540g Nutella
340g mascarpone
A pinch of salt
100 grams of ground and roasted hazelnuts, coconut flakes, chocolate flakes or almond flakes

METHOD OF PREPARATION:
How to prepare the crust

Preheat the oven to 180 C.
Combine the crushed biscuits with the salt powder and melted butter and mix well. Press well the composition obtained on the bottom of a tray with a diameter of 23 cm, greased with butter or lined with baking paper.
Put it in the oven for 10 minutes, then take it out and let it cool completely.

How to prepare the cream

With an electric mixer, mix Nutella with mascarpone and salt powder at medium speed until well blended and fluffy.
Place the composition over the biscuit crust, cover everything with a plastic wrap and leave it to cool for an hour.
Before serving, put the crushed hazelnuts on it.

Good appetite!

Chocolate brownie and mascarpone

BROWNIE INGREDIENTS WITH CHOCOLATE AND MASCARPONE

220 grams of butter

90 grams of dark chocolate

210 grams of granulated sugar

65 grams of cocoa

110 grams of mascarpone

3 large eggs at room temperature

65 grams of flour

2 teaspoons vanilla flavor

GLAZING INGREDIENTS

170 grams of chocolate

6 tablespoons whipped cream

40 grams of unsalted butter

METHOD OF PREPARATION:

Preheat the oven to 180 degrees Celsius and grease a 20 cm tray with butter or line it with baking paper.

Melt the broken chocolate pieces and butter cut into cubes over very low heat, in a bowl with a thick bottom or put the bowl in a saucepan with water over low heat. After they have completely melted, mix them until they are homogeneous. Add the cocoa and sugar and mix.

In another bowl, beat the mascarpone cream, eggs and vanilla until smooth. Add the flour and salt and mix well.

Then pour the chocolate cream over the mascarpone cream and pour the composition into the pan.

Leave it in the oven for 45–50 minutes or until it passes the toothpick test. After removing it from the oven, let it cool.

In the meantime, you can take care of the glaze. Break the chocolate into small pieces. Cut the butter into cubes and put the cream in a bowl with a thick bottom over low heat and stir continuously. When the mixture almost starts to boil, add the chopped chocolate. Let it sit for 30 seconds, then stir until smooth.

Pour the icing evenly over the grated parchment.

Allow the icing to harden before cutting the cake. You can even put it in the cold for an hour.

Good appetite!

The simplest brownie recipe. It is made from only two ingredients

The simplest brownie recipe. You don't even need flour, sugar or baking powder. It is made from only two ingredients and you don't even have to spend too much time in the kitchen. So, you don't need a sheet of paper and a pencil to write down your ingredients, because all you need is a chocolate spread and 4 eggs and you will get the simplest and fastest cake.

No one will believe you prepared it in just 10 minutes. It doesn't take long. According to Tasty Kitchen, the only secret is to beat the eggs well, until they almost triple in volume. This way you will get a brownie like in magazines, with a "chocolate" interior and a crispy crust on the surface.

THE EASIEST BROWNIE RECIPE. INGREDIENTS
4 eggs,
240g spreadable chocolate cream

METHOD OF PREPARATION:
Prepare a baking tray (20x20cm) and line it with baking paper.

Beat the eggs in a frying pan for 8-10 minutes, until they triple in volume.
Heat the spreadable chocolate cream a little by keeping it in a bowl with hot water or in the microwave for 1 minute, stirring every 15 seconds.

Incorporate the spreadable chocolate cream into the beaten eggs, using the mixer on low speed. Mix several times in the dough formed with a silicone spatula.
Pour the composition into the prepared tray and bake for 25-30 minutes in the oven heated to 180 C.

Brownie is ready when it starts to come off easily from the walls of the tray or if it passes the toothpick test.

Let the brownie cool completely before removing it from the pan. It can be served with a glass of ice cream.

Good appetite!

Traditional Easter with dough, sweet cheese and raisins

Do you dare to prepare a traditional Easter with cake–like dough, stuffed with sweet cheese and raisins soaked in rum? You won't find a recipe easier to follow than this!

Dough INGREDIENTS
280 g flour
130 ml of milk
100 g butter
50 g raisins
50 g sugar
1 or
1 teaspoon dried yeast
vanilla essence
rum essence
the peel of a lemon

a generous salt powder

2 tablespoons oil

INGREDIENTS FOR CHEESE FILLING

500 g of cottage cheese

2 eggs

10 tablespoons sugar

vanilla essence

rum essence

150 g fermented sour cream

150 g raisins

100 ml rom

100 g flour

COOKING INGREDIENTS

1 or

2 tablespoons milk

METHOD OF PREPARATION:

1. Dissolve the yeast and sugar in the slightly warm milk and set aside the yeast for 10 minutes to activate.

2. Meanwhile, beat the soft butter with the egg, then add the yeast.

3. Incorporate the flour combined with the salt into the liquid ingredients and add the washed raisins.

4. Knead the dough for 15 minutes in a mixer or 20 minutes by hand, until you get a fine and non-sticky dough.

5. Grease a bowl with oil and let the dough rise in it, covered with plastic wrap, for about 2 hours.

6. For the filling, let the raisins soak in rum for 20–30 minutes before preparing the filling.

7. Then combine the ingredients for the filling with a mixer, draining the rum raisins well.

8. When the dough has risen, divide it in 2 and spread half of the dough on a well-floured countertop.

9. Place the dough sheet in a cake pan greased with butter and leave to rise.

10. Spread the rest of the crust and form the "walls" of the Easter tray, stretching the crust long and cutting the excess that comes out of the tray.

11. After making sure that the two layers of crust are glued together, pour the cheese filling into the tray.

12. From the excess dough cut from the edge of the tray, decorate the Easter on the center, either in a cross or with a braid. Grease the traditional Easter egg with beaten milk before putting it in the oven.

13. Let the pasca rise for at least 30 minutes in the heat, then bake it at 180 degrees for 50–55 minutes, or until browned and stabilized in the center.

Good appetite!

Glazed check with lemon and poppy seeds

How do you prepare a cake glazed with lemon and poppy in abundance? Follow this recipe and you get the tastiest and most flavorful homemade dessert, ready in a short time and with a minimum of ingredients!

INGREDIENTS FOR CHECK
280 g flour
150 g sugar
4 tablespoons poppy seeds
250 ml milk
2 eggs
1 teaspoon baking powder
a baking soda knife tip
vanilla essence

the peel of a lemon
100 g butter
a pinch of salt

INGREDIENTS FOR LEMON GLAZING
150 g powdered sugar
the juice of a lemon

METHOD OF PREPARATION:

1. Combine flour with granulated sugar, baking soda, baking powder, a generous pinch of salt and poppy seeds.
2. Separately, beat eggs with melted butter, milk, vanilla essence and lemon peel.
3. Incorporate the dry ingredients into the liquid ones, until you get a homogeneous dough.
4. Pour the cake composition with lemon and poppy seeds into a cake tin lined with baking sheet.
5. Shape in a preheated oven at 180 degrees for 55 minutes, or until browned and passed the toothpick test.
6. Meanwhile, to get the lemon glaze, beat the lemon juice with the powdered sugar.
7. After removing the cake with lemon and poppy seeds from the oven, spread the icing on top and serve the cake after cooling.

Good appetite!

Sticky blackberry with chocolate

Do you know that black woman that my grandmother prepared, which seemed to have a icing poured on top and a rich taste, even if it wasn't difficult at all, in a multitude of stages? This is exactly how this sticky blackberry comes out, prepared with plenty of dark chocolate!

INGREDIENTS

230 g dark chocolate

a spoon with black cocoa tip

1 tablespoon instant coffee

300 g butter

400 g sugar

100 g brown sugar

2 teaspoons vanilla essence

a generous salt powder

6 eggs
 150 g flour
 50 g black cocoa

METHOD OF PREPARATION:

1. Grease a tray with butter and line the tray with baking paper, then grease the baking paper on top.
2. Combine dark chocolate with a tablespoon of dark cocoa and a tablespoon of instant coffee, and pour the melted butter completely over them.
3. Set the chocolate mixture aside for a few minutes.
4. Separately, combine the 2 types of sugar, vanilla essence and salt powder. Then incorporate the 6 eggs in a row and combine them with the mixer for a few good minutes, until the composition swells.
5. Once the fluffy dough is obtained, incorporate the chocolate icing set aside.
6. Then incorporate the flour and 50 g of flour with a spatula, so as not to deflate the eggs. Pour the composition into the pan and level it.
7. Bake the sticky blackberry for 45–50 minutes in the oven at 180 degrees.
8. Remember that in the case of this blackberry recipe, you cannot check if it is penetrated with the toothpick, because it must remain sticky.

Good appetite!

Magic cheesecake

Do you remember Magic Cake or Intelligence? It caused a stir last year on the internet. The same principle can be applied to get a delicious magic cheesecake! Pour a single dough into the tray and, surprise !, you get 2 distinct layers, one creamy, another fluffy!

INGREDIENTS

300 g cream cheese
100 g of sugar
vanilla essence
6 yolks
120 g flour
400 ml of milk
6 egg whites
a pinch of salt
100 g of sugar
a few drops of vinegar

METHOD OF PREPARATION:

1. Beat the cream cheese with 100 g sugar and vanilla essence for 2-3 minutes. Gradually add the yolks, then incorporate the flour and milk.

2. Separately, beat the egg whites with 4-5 drops of vinegar and a pinch of salt. Gradually add 100 g of sugar and beat the egg whites until they stick well (7-8 min).

3. Incorporate the egg whites into the initial dough and pour the composition into a cake tin lined with baking sheet.

4. Put the magic cheesecake in the oven at 150 degrees for 50-55 minutes, or until it stabilizes and browns (do not open the oven in the first 30 minutes of baking).

5. Let the magic cheesecake cool for at least 2 hours before serving.

Good appetite!

Kinder Pingui cake

Do you love the fluffy dessert with milk, what melts in your mouth? It is not difficult at all to prepare it at home! Here's how to have a Kinder Pingui cake to share with your loved ones, fast and delicious.

Dough INGREDIENTS
3 eggs
30 g cocoa
30 g flour
40 g sugar
vanilla essence
1 teaspoon lemon juice
a pinch of salt

CREAM INGREDIENTS
 500 g mascarpone
 250 g whipped cream
 130 g old powder
 vanilla essence

GLAZING INGREDIENTS
 300 g chocolate
 4 tablespoons oil
 2 tablespoons sugar

METHOD OF PREPARATION:
1. Separate the eggs and beat the egg whites with a pinch of salt and lemon juice until they foam and stick to the target.
2. Separately, beat the yolks with the sugar and vanilla essence until you get a light and fluffy cream.
3. Incorporate the egg whites into the yolks with a spatula, then incorporate the flour combined with the cocoa.
4. Once you get a homogeneous consistency, spread it in a large tray, lined with baking sheet. Put the tray in the oven for 12–15 minutes at 180 degrees.
5. While the countertop cools, prepare the cream: Beat the mascarpone for 3-4 minutes, then incorporate the whipping cream and add the sugar and vanilla essence.
6. Cut the top into 3 equal pieces and place a first piece in a cake pan or heat resistant.

7. Spread 1/2 of the cream on top. Add the second layer, followed by the rest of the cream and the third layer of top.

8. Melt the chocolate with the oil and 2 tablespoons of sugar in a bain marie or in the microwave, in rounds of 30 seconds followed by mixing.

9. Spread the chocolate over the Kinder Pingui cake. Let the cake cool for at least an hour before serving.

Good appetite!

Shadow chocolate cake (in gradients)

Do you want to make a good impression in front of all the guests? With a shadow chocolate cake, that is in gradients, you will leave a mask to everyone and they will guarantee you a guaranteed recipe!

The dessert is not drowning at all, but on the contrary, it is fluffy and melts in your mouth at the same time!

INGREDIENTS
25 g black cocoa
150 g + 50 g sugar
50 ml of boiling water
vanilla essence
a baking soda powder
220 g flour

1 sachet of baking powder
1 pinch of salt
250 g soft butter
4 husband eggs
80 ml milk

METHOD OF PREPARATION:

1. Combine boiling water with black cocoa, 50 g sugar, vanilla essence and baking soda.
2. Separately, combine the flour with the baking powder and a pinch of salt and set aside.
3. Beat the soft butter for 5-7 minutes with the rest of the sugar, until you get a fluffy consistency, then incorporate the eggs one by one and beat the dough well after each addition.
4. Finally, sift and incorporate the dry ingredients at low speed, then add the milk. Pour about a third of the dough over the chocolate icing obtained and mix well.
5. Pour the first layer of chocolate cake in gradients in a cake pan lined with baking sheet, keeping about 3 tablespoons of the composition aside.
6. Over the 3 tablespoons of the preserved composition, add another third of the dough and mix well.
7. Spread the lighter dough obtained also in the tray, with a spatula, to avoid the combination of colors, then level carefully.
8. Finally, pour the last third of the remaining composition over the two layers of dough, spreading it very carefully with a spatula.

9. Level the chocolate cake in the shade and put it in the oven at 180 degrees for 60 minutes, or until the cake passes the toothpick test.

Good appetite!

Basbousa semolina cake

A delicacy of syrup cake in semolina, of oriental origin, which you will surely love! Look how easy you prepare it and then find out how quickly it disappears from the serving platter!

INGREDIENTS

400 g gray
150 g sugar
1 sachet of baking powder
100 g coconut flakes
2 eggs husband
150 g butter
250 g yogurt
vanilla essence
100 g almonds

INGREDIENTS FOR SYRUP

400 g sugar
500 ml of water
1 teaspoon lemon juice

METHOD OF PREPARATION:

1. Combine the sugar with the lemon juice and lemon juice, then boil them until the sugar has completely dissolved.
2. Separately, combine the dry ingredients: semolina, sugar, baking powder and coconut flakes.
3. Then incorporate the rest of the ingredients (eggs, yogurt, vanilla essence) and pour the composition obtained in an oven tray richly greased with butter.
4. Spread the composition and refrigerate for 2 hours. After 2 hours, draw the squares of the Basbousa semolina cake with a knife and place an almond in the center of each square.
5. Bake the cake at 190 degrees for 40 minutes, or until evenly browned.
6. When you take the semolina cake out of the oven, syrup it immediately, then put it in the oven for another 15 minutes.

Good appetite!

Cake with sheets and chocolate cream

Regardless of whether you call it the cake with sheets and chocolate cream or Snow White with chocolate, the cake is the same, and the recipe is guaranteed! It comes out tender and creamy, a combination that will quickly disappear from the plate!

INGREDIENTS FOR SHEETS

1 or

a teaspoon of ammonia

2 teaspoons vinegar

6 tablespoons oil

5 tablespoons milk

6 tablespoons sugar

flour, as it contains

INGREDIENTS FOR CHOCOLATE CREAM

700 ml whole milk

6 tablespoons sugar

3 tablespoons starch

2 tablespoons cocoa

200 g dark chocolate

1/2 teaspoon rom essence – optional

METHOD OF PREPARATION:

Preparation of chocolate cream

1. First prepare the chocolate cream for the sheet cake and the chocolate cream, so that it has time to cool completely before assembling the cake.

2. Boil 3/4 of the milk, keeping the rest aside. Combine the rest of the milk with the sugar, starch and cocoa mixed separately and mix until you get a fine paste.

3. When the milk boils, pour the paste obtained over the milk, turn on low heat and continue to mix in the chocolate cream until it thickens.

4. Once the fire is extinguished, add the diced or cut chocolate, then mix again until the chocolate is completely melted.

Preparing the sheets for the chocolate cake

1. Combine all the ingredients for the sheets, except the flour and mix until you get a homogeneous mixture.

2. Incorporate the flour little by little, in large tranches initially, then decrease the amount of flour added as the dough begins to thicken.

3. When the dough no longer sticks to your hand, but remains greasy, do not add flour. Divide the dough into 5–6 equal pieces and spread the sheets on baking sheets or directly on the bottom of the tray.

4. Bake the tray for 4–5 minutes for each sheet.

5. When all the sheets are ready and the cream has cooled, alternate the cake sheets with the cream, and on top decorate the cake with grated chocolate or cocoa. Put the cake with sheets and chocolate in the fridge with a weight on top (wood chopper) and leave it to cool for at least 8 hours before serving.

Good appetite!

Snow White cake with coconut cream

Snow White cake is not as complicated as you might imagine! Although it is a sheet cake, it will surely come out great at first, if you follow this recipe.

INGREDIENTS FOR SHEETS
1 or
a teaspoon of ammonia
2 teaspoons vinegar
6 tablespoons oil
5 tablespoons milk
6 tablespoons sugar
flour, as it contains

INGREDIENTS FOR COCONUT CREAM
750 ml milk
5 tablespoons coconut
8 tablespoons sugar
3 tablespoons starch
100 g butter

ORNAMENTAL INGREDIENTS
coconut flakes

METHOD OF PREPARATION:
Prepare coconut cream:

1. Put most of the milk to boil in a non-stick pan, keeping about 5-6 tablespoons in a bowl.

2. In the preserved milk, add the coconut and starch. Combine everything until you get a homogeneous and dense mixture.

3. When the milk is boiling, turn on low heat and add the starch mixture. Stir continuously or every few minutes to avoid sticking to the pan. When the cream thickens, remove from the heat, add the butter, mix and leave to cool.

Prepare the dough for sheets:
1. Quench the ammonia in 2 teaspoons of vinegar, add the egg, sugar, 5 tablespoons of milk and the 6 tablespoons of oil. Then gradually incorporate the flour, more at first, and as the dough

groups, add in smaller portions.

2. When the dough no longer sticks to the kneading hands, do not add flour at all.

3. Depending on the tray you will use for the sheets, divide the dough into 4-5-6 equal pieces.

✳ The Snow White cake in the pictures was made of 6 sheets, baked on the bottom of a round tray, with a diameter of 26 cm.

4. Spread thinly and as evenly as possible one of the parts of the dough on the bottom of a tray, lightly lined with flour. Bake the sheet for 5-7 minutes, or until the sheet begins to brown slightly.
5. Remove the baked sheet on a serving platter, place a layer of coconut cream on top of it and prepare the next sheet.

6. Do the same with all the other pieces of dough, until you finish baking the sheets.

7. Keep a little cream to spread over the last sheet. Sift coconut flakes over the cream layer and refrigerate the cake for 12 hours or overnight, covered with a baking sheet, over which you place a mincer or other medium weight, to keep the cake sheets in contact with the cream.
✳ NB !: Do not try to cut the Snow White cake earlier than 12 hours! Cakes made of ammonia are hydrophilic and need a rest period to soften and swell.
Good appetite!

Christmas cake with dried fruits and nuts

Do you want to prepare the most fragrant dessert for Christmas? Try a delicious cake filled with dried fruits and nuts, a delicacy with which you are guaranteed to surprise your guests.

Dough INGREDIENTS
200 g flour
200 g butter (one pack)
3 eggs
200 g brown sugar
vanilla essence
1 teaspoon baking powder
a pinch of salt
3 tablespoons milk

INGREDIENTS FOR FRUIT AND WALNUT MIX:

50 g cashews

50 g almonds

100 g candied figs

100 g candied cherries

100 g raisins

the peel of an orange

a generous cinnamon powder

a clove powder

a nutmeg powder

METHOD OF PREPARATION:

1. Combine all dried fruit with walnuts (cashews, almonds) and spices, then set aside.
2. Separately, beat the butter with the sugar for 5–7 minutes, until you get a very fine cream, then add one egg at a time, followed by the vanilla essence.
3. Incorporate flour combined with baking powder and salt, then incorporate milk.
4. Add the dried fruits and nuts, keeping a few to place on top.
5. Spread the Christmas cake composition with dried fruit in a tray lined with oil and flour, then bake it for 80–90 minutes at 160 degrees, or until the Christmas cake passes the toothpick test.
6. Serve the dessert powdered with sugar and decorated to taste.

Good appetite!

Homemade cake with cottage cheese and apricots

It is refreshing, rich in fruit and full enough to keep you hungry, if you serve it as a snack! Homemade cake with cottage cheese and apricots is easy to prepare by anyone, regardless of the level of experience in the kitchen and is a summer delight that you must try!

INGREDIENTS

1 kg of fat cow's cheese

5 eggs

7 tablespoons gray

150 g sugar

200 ml of milk

vanilla essence

500 g sour cream

lemon / orange peel

1/2 teaspoon baking powder
a pinch of salt
8–9 fresh or dried apricots

METHOD OF PREPARATION:

1. If you are going to prepare the cake with cottage cheese and apricots with dried fruits, hydrate them for 20 minutes in rum or milk before preparing the cake.

2. Beat the cream cheese with the eggs, sour cream, sugar and spices. Add the semolina, baking powder and a pinch of salt, then mix well until smooth.

3. Pour the composition for the cake with cottage cheese and apricots in a tray lined with butter, then pour the composition and level it.

4. Insert clean or hydrated apricot slices into the level composition, in case of dry ones.

5. Place the pan in the preheated oven at 170 degrees for 45–50 minutes, or until the cake has swelled considerably and lightly browned on top. Cut the cake with cottage cheese and diced apricots and serve cold.

Good appetite!

Peach Cobbler – Peach Cobbler

The peach cobbler is an atypical cake, a delicious hybrid between a pancake prepared in the oven and a fluffy peach cake.

It comes out a combination that you can hardly describe, a perfect dessert for mid-summer, when the peaches are well ripened and sweet. But nothing says that you can not prepare this dessert even with the arrival of winter, if you use peaches in compote.

INGREDIENTS
1 kg of peaches
1/2 teaspoon cinnamon
the juice of a lemon
100 g of sugar

Dough INGREDIENTS

150 g flour

100 g butter

2 teaspoons baking powder

a pinch of salt

200 g sugar

1 or

200 milk

vanilla essence

METHOD OF PREPARATION:

1. Wash and cut sliced peaches (you can also use peaches from compote, in which case it is no longer necessary to cut them).
2. Combine the peaches, sugar and cinnamon in a saucepan and heat over medium heat. Mix well, until the sugar melts and let the composition boil, until the peaches are syrupy.
3. Separately, combine the dry ingredients for the dough: flour, sugar, baking powder, salt powder.
4. Add egg, milk, vanilla essence and mix until smooth. The result should be a pancake-like dough.
5. Pour the melted butter completely into an oven or heat-resistant pan.
6. Pour the dough over the butter, but without stirring it a little.
7. Place the peaches with the syrup over the cobbler dough, being careful not to mix them too much with the dough.

8. Place the pan with the peach cobbler in the oven at 180 degrees for 45–50 minutes. Serve the cobbler with peaches after cooling, with 1–2 cups of vanilla ice cream on top.

Good appetite!

Cake with strawberries and mascarpone cream

Do you want to prepare a summer dessert? Try a creamy and fruity cake with strawberries and mascarpone, a fluffy and strong, very fragrant delight!

TABLE INGREDIENTS
70 g butter
6 tablespoons milk
10 tablespoons sugar
12 tablespoons flour
6 eggs
1 teaspoon lemon juice
a pinch of salt

TABLE INGREDIENTS

70 g butter

6 tablespoons milk

10 tablespoons sugar

12 tablespoons flour

6 eggs

1 teaspoon lemon juice

a pinch of salt

INGREDIENTS FOR STRAWBERRY CREAM

200 g mascarpone cheese

100 ml whipped cream

3 tablespoons powdered sugar

1 teaspoon vanilla essence

4–5 strawberries

ORNAMENTAL INGREDIENTS

250 g strawberries

2 sachets of gelatin

200 ml + 2 tablespoons water

2 tablespoons sugar

METHOD OF PREPARATION:

Preparing the top for the cake with strawberries and mascarpone cream

1. Melt the butter and mix it with the salt, milk and 2 tablespoons of sugar, then incorporate the flour. Separate the eggs and bring the yolks over the butter cream obtained.

2. Separately, beat the egg whites with the remaining sugar, a pinch of salt and lemon juice, until they stick well to the target.

3. Incorporate the first composition in the second until homogeneous, using a wire or a spatula, being careful not to remove air from the egg whites.

4. Pour the dough obtained in a cake pan lined with baking sheet and put the tray in the oven in a water bath, in another larger tray, at 140 degrees, for an hour, or until the top is browned and it is completely solidified. Let it cool in the oven off.

5. When the countertop cools, remove it from the tray and cut it 2 into equal countertops

Preparing the cream + assembling the cake with strawberries and mascarpone cheese

1. Beat mascarpone cheese with whipped cream, vanilla and sugar. Then add a few diced strawberries.

2. Assemble the cake in the tray in which you initially baked the top:

3. Hydrate the gelatin with 2-3 tablespoons of water and set aside for 10 minutes.

4. Spread half of the cream between the two layers of countertop, and the other half of the amount of cream, over the strawberry cake.

5. On top of the second layer of cream, place the chopped strawberries / cubes in a messy way.

6. Put the hydrated gelatin in the microwave for 15-20 seconds, until it dissolves. Then mix it with the syrup obtained from the rest of the water, heated with the sugar until the latter has melted.
7. Pour the gelatin over the fruit placed on top of the strawberry and mascarpone cream cake, then refrigerate the dessert for at least 2 hours, or until the cake has completely solidified.

Good appetite!

Strawberry cheesecake

The period of strawberries is so short that you want to eat them in all forms. Try the best strawberry cheesecake, a dessert as good-looking as it is easy to prepare! You don't even have to turn on the oven for it.

INGREDIENTS
 200 g simple biscuits
 80 g butter
 1 tablespoon sugar

CREAM INGREDIENTS
 500 g mascarpone
 200 ml whipped cream

150 g yogurt
4 + 2 tablespoons sugar
vanilla essence
500 g strawberries
2 sachets of gelatin
the water

METHOD OF PREPARATION:

Crush the biscuits as finely as possible, in the food processor or in a bag, using a spatula. Combine the biscuits with the melted butter and a spoonful of sugar, then press them into a cake tin with removable walls. Put the tray in the freezer while you prepare the cream.

Combine a sachet of gelatin with 2 tablespoons of water and set aside to hydrate. Mix mascarpone with cream and whipped cream. Add 4 tablespoons sugar and vanilla essence.

Wash the strawberries well (keeping a few for decoration) and grind them in a blender with 2 glasses of cold water. Add 1/3 of the liquid from the blender over the mascarpone cream, straining it. Put hydrated gelatin in the composition and mix quickly. Pour the strawberry cream over the biscuit top and refrigerate the cake for at least 2 hours, or until it solidifies completely.

After the cake has hardened, moisturize the other gelatin sachet. Add 2 tablespoons of sugar over the remaining strawberry juice in a blender and mix again.

Strain the strawberries, combine them with hydrated gelatin and pour this juice over the entire surface of the cake. Cut the preserved strawberries in half or slices and place them in the juice layer. Let the cake cool until it solidifies (minimum 2 hours).

Good appetite!

Cheesecake with Nutella and strawberries

Easy to make and refreshing, the cheesecake with Nutella and strawberries is perfect to be served on a hot summer day.

INGREDIENTS

150 g biscuits with cocoa

60 g melted butter

1 kg of cream cheese at room temperature

250 g sour cream

250 ml condensed milk

vanilla essence

1 small jar of Nutella or other chocolate cream with hazelnuts

1 sachet of gelatin
2 tablespoons water
300 g strawberries

METHOD OF PREPARATION:

Preheat the oven to 180 degrees and line a narrow, high cake pan with baking paper. Grind the biscuits in the food processor, mix them with the melted butter and press the composition in the tray, then put it in the oven for 10 minutes.

Beat the cream cheese for 10 minutes, add the cream, condensed milk, vanilla and melted chocolate cream in the microwave. Mix the gelatin with water and heat it for 30–40 seconds, then pour it over the cream and continue mixing.

Put 1/2 composition in the pan, chop and arrange 1/2 of the amount of strawberries, place the rest of the cream in the pan and refrigerate for 5 hours. Before serving, remove the cheesecake from the pan and remove with

knife on the edge, then garnish it with strawberries cut into slices or halves.

Good appetite!

Cabana Cake (Roofing)

Dough INGREDIENTS

400 g flour

a pinch of salt

1 sachet of baking powder

50 g powdered sugar

250 g thick cream

250 g butter / margarine

CREAM INGREDIENTS (OPTIONAL)

200 g butter

400 g sweet milk (caramel)

ORNAMENTAL INGREDIENTS

200 ml fresh

6-7 tablespoons chopped walnuts / hazelnuts

METHOD OF PREPARATION:

Preparing the dough for the Roof / Cottage Cake

1. Combine flour with salt powder, baking powder and powdered sugar. Homogenize the dry ingredients, then add the sour cream and incorporate the soft margarine.
2. Knead for 7-10 minutes, or until you get a fairly homogeneous dough, but still soft.
3. Pour the dough on a food foil, give it a square shape and refrigerate for at least 3 hours.

Preparing the "sticks" for the Roof / Cottage Cake

1. Once removed from the fridge, roll out the dough on the baking sheet and cut it into 15 equal pieces.
2. Keep one of the pieces outside, and put the remaining 14 in the fridge until you work with them.
3. Roll the piece of dough kept between the palms and the top, until you get a long stick and just as thick everywhere.
4. Place the dough stick between 2 baking sheets and spread it on a thin sheet, about a palm wide. Place fresh cherries or sour cherries, without seeds, on the edge of the dough sheet.
5. Roll the dough over the cherries carefully, until you get a long stick.
6. Repeat the same procedure with all the other 14 pieces of dough, rolling them and filling them with cherries.
7. Place the sticks spaced apart (in 2 different rounds, if they don't all fit at once) in a tray lined with baking sheet and bake for ~ 20 minutes at 200 degrees, or until the sticks are nicely browned.

Preparing the cream for the Roof / Cottage Cake

1. Beat the butter with dulce de leche for 6–7 minutes, or until you get a light cream. Refrigerate the cream for at least 2 hours.

2. Place 5 ripe sticks, filled with cherries, on a serving tray. Grease them with caramel cream and level the cream layer.

3. Place another 4 sticks on top, add another layer of cream, followed by a layer of 3, 2 and 1 stick, each time adding a layer of caramel cream.

4. After you have added the last stick, coat the cake in whipped cream and sprinkle the hazelnuts or walnuts cut with a knife over the roof cake.

Alternatively, if you don't like the taste of caramel, you can "assemble" the cake using a little more whipped cream.

Good appetite!

Cherry cheesecake

Cherry cheesecake is one of the most creamy and refined desserts you can prepare, right at home, according to this recipe. You do it from 0 in 3 simple steps and you can't go wrong!

INGREDIENTS FOR CHEESECAKE COUNTER
200 g simple biscuits

80 g butter

INGREDIENTS FOR THE CHEESE LAYER
500 g cream cheese

180 g sugar

200 g sour cream

150 ml whipped cream

2 eggs
2 tablespoons starch
vanilla essence
a teaspoon of lemon juice

INGREDIENTS FOR CHERRY TOPPING

2 tablespoons starch
400 g seedless cherries
250 ml water
100 g of sugar

METHOD OF PREPARATION:

Preparation of the cheesecake top with cherries
1. Crush the biscuits as finely as possible and combine them with the 80 g melted butter. Place this composition in a cake pan with removable walls, wallpaper with baking paper and press the mixture well into the pan.
2. Wrap the bottom of the tray in aluminum foil to insulate it from the water in which it will sit in the oven.

Prepare the cream cheese layer
1. Beat the cream cheese with the sugar for 4-5 minutes, then add the vanilla essence, sour cream, whipped cream, the two eggs, lemon juice, vanilla essence and starch.

2. Homogenize the composition well and pour it into the tray, then level the surface and put the tray in the oven, in another tray, larger, with water, for 30 minutes at 180 degrees and for another 30 minutes at 150 degrees. grade.

3. After turning off the oven, leave the cherry cheesecake in the oven for another hour, with the door closed.

Meanwhile, prepare the layer of cherries:

1. Bring the cleaned cherries to a boil, together with 2/3 of the amount of water. In the rest of the water, dissolve the starch and sugar.

2. Once the cherries start to boil, add the water with starch and sugar and, from this point, stir continuously for the next 8-10 minutes.

3. Turn off the heat and continue to stir. Initially, the cherry sauce will become cloudy and pasty in color, and then become transparent and glossy.

4. Serve each slice of cheesecake with 1-2 tablespoons of cherry sauce on top.

Good appetite!

Pineapple cheesecake

Sweet, exotic and very presentable: look how simple it is to make a pineapple cheeesecake, garnished with a layer of delicious jelly on top.

TABLE INGREDIENTS
 200 g of champagne biscuits
 120 g butter

INGREDIENTS FOR PINEAPPLE CREAM
 2 sachets of gelatin
 300 g cream cheese
 250 g fresh
 200 ml pineapple juice
 3 teaspoons lemon juice
 100 g of sugar
 1 tablespoon starch
 200 g pineapple pieces

INGREDIENTS FOR THE JELLY LAYER
 250 ml pineapple juice
 1 sachet of gelatin

METHOD OF PREPARATION:

Preparing the cheesecake top
1. Chop the champagne biscuits in the food processor, then combine them with the melted butter.

2. Press the mixture obtained in a cake tray about 26 cm in diameter.

Preparation of pineapple cream
1. Hydrate the two sachets of gelatin with 2-3 tablespoons of water and set aside until they swell (about 10 minutes).
2. Meanwhile, combine the pineapple juice with the lemon juice, sugar and starch. Mix well and simmer the mixture until the mixture becomes uniform and thickens slightly.

3. Turn off the heat and let the mixture cool a little. Add hydrated gelatin, mix as well as possible and let it cool a little more (about 10 minutes).

4. Incorporate the cream cheese into the pineapple sauce, then add the whipped cream and the pineapple pieces. Pour the composition obtained over the biscuit top, level it and put the cheesecake in the fridge for an hour.

Preparation of pineapple jelly

1. Soak the gelatin sachet in 2 tablespoons of water and leave for 10 minutes.

2. Heat the pineapple juice for 4–5 minutes, then add the swollen gelatin. After it cools, add the pineapple juice over the cheesecake and put it back in the fridge, ideally overnight.

3. Serve the pineapple cheesecake served with whipped cream and pineapple pieces.

Good appetite!

Cheesecake with Oreo cookies without oven

Here's how to make a cheesecake with Oreo cookies without an oven, ideal for summer days when you don't feel like lighting a fire. Super fast and easy to do!

INGREDIENTS

3 packs of large Oreo biscuits

225 g soft cream cheese

50 g sugar

vanilla essence

200 g liquid cream

5 tablespoons soft butter

METHOD OF PREPARATION:

Grind 20–25 Oreo biscuits in a grinder, or grind them manually in a bag drilled at one point, using a spatula.

After you have ground the biscuits well, add the butter and mix well, then press the crust obtained in the tray in which you will make the cheesecake. Let the pan cool for 30 minutes.

Beat the cream cheese together with the sugar and vanilla essence using a mixer. Add 8 broken Oreo biscuits into smaller pieces. Add the whipped cream, but keep a little for garnish.

Put the filling obtained in the tray in which you cooled the crust and garnish with the remaining whipped cream, then break 2–3 Oreo biscuits and sprinkle them over the cheesecake.

Good appetite!

"Danube Waves" cake with cherries and chocolate

It is a very famous cake and can be prepared all year round! Danube Waves cake can also be prepared with compote or sour cherry cherries, which makes it perfect, regardless of the season.

TABLE INGREDIENTS
250 g butter
200 g sugar
1 sachet of vanilla sugar
5 eggs
380 g flour
1 sachet of baking powder
2 tablespoons cocoa
1 tablespoon milk

FRUIT LAYER INGREDIENTS

700 g pitted cherries

3 tablespoons sugar

1 sachet of vanilla sugar

INGREDIENTS FOR VANILLA CREAM

1 sachet of vanilla pudding

500 ml of milk

100 g of sugar

200 g soft butter

INGREDIENTS FOR CHOCOLATE GLAZING

200 g dark chocolate

2 tablespoons oil

METHOD OF PREPARATION:

Danube Waves Cake – Countertop preparation

1. Combine sugar with soft butter and vanilla sugar, then mix for 3–5 minutes. Add eggs one at a time. Incorporate flour mixed with baking powder and mix until smooth.

2. Separate 1/3 of the composition and mix it with cocoa and a tablespoon of milk until smooth.

3. In an oven tray greased with butter and lined with flour, spread the remaining white composition and level it as well as possible. Above it spreads the composition layer with cocoa.

4. Over the cocoa layer, spread the pitted cherries (they can also be made of compote!), Mixed with sugar and vanilla sugar.
5. Bake the cake for 40 minutes at 180 degrees, or until the cake passes the toothpick test.

Danube Waves Cake – Preparation of vanilla cream
1. In time, prepare the vanilla pudding: combine 100 ml of milk with 100 g of sugar and the contents of a bag of pudding.
2. Bring the milk to a boil, and when it boils, add the pudding composition and stir constantly, until the cream thickens, then leave it to cool.
3. Beat the soft butter with the mixer for at least 5 minutes, then gradually incorporate the vanilla pudding prepared earlier.
4. Spread the vanilla cream obtained over the layer of cherries, level and put the cake in the freezer for 10–15 minutes.

Danube Waves Cake – Preparation of chocolate icing
1. Melt the chocolate with the oil and spread the icing obtained over the vanilla layer.
2. Serve the Danube Waves cake with chocolate after two hours of refrigeration.

Good appetite!

Cream Cream – Cream with vanilla cream

Do you love to enjoy a creamy vanilla with a rich and creamy taste? Prepare it at home! Cremes cake, as it is also called, is child's play to prepare if you have the right recipe!

INGREDIENTS

1 packet foiled
8 eggs
300 g sugar
1L + 100 ml milk
100 g flour
2 tablespoons starch
2 sachets of powdered sugar
vanilla essence
200 ml fresh

METHOD OF PREPARATION:

Prepare Cremsnit sheets:
1. Thaw the package of foil and divide it into two equal parts. Spread each half as well as possible on a suitable baking tray.

2. Grease the oven tray and place one of the two sides of the spreadsheet, then cut it well with a fork over the entire surface to prevent it from growing.

3. Bake the foil for about 12 minutes at 200 degrees, or until nicely browned. Remove the first part of the foil and put the next sheet in the oven, superficially growing large squares, delimiting the portions of Cremsnit.

4. Bake the foil for another 12 minutes at 200 degrees or until the second half browns nicely.

Then prepare the vanilla cream for Cremsnit:
1. Separate the yolks from the whites. Rub the yolks with half the amount of sugar (150 g), starch, flour and 100 ml of milk for 5–10 minutes.

2. Separately, beat the egg whites with a pinch of salt, then with the remaining sugar (150 g), until they stick to the container. Put 1 L of milk to boil with vanilla sugar.

3. When the milk boils, take it with a polish and pour over the yolk mixture. Stir quickly and vigorously to prevent the yolks from clotting.

4. Repeat the procedure to bring the yolk cream to a temperature close to that of the milk, then you can pour the whole composition over the milk, in the pan.

5. Stir constantly over medium heat until the vanilla cream for Cremsnit begins to thicken, then remove from the heat.

6. Immediately incorporate the well-beaten egg whites, using a spatula and movements from bottom to top. Let the cream cool a little, then incorporate in the same way the whipped cream.

7. Spread the composition obtained over the first baked Cremsnit sheet. Level well and place the second sheet on top of it, then refrigerate the cake for at least 3-4 hours.

8. Cut the cream with vanilla cream using the notched lines before baking and serve the cake cold.

Good appetite!

NOTES

NOTES

_____

_____

_____

_____

_____

_____

_____

_____

_____

_____

NOTES

NOTES

_____

_____

_____

_____

_____

_____

_____

_____

_____

_____

_____

NOTES

_____

_____

_____

_____

_____

_____

_____

_____

_____

_____

_____

NOTES

_____

_____

_____

_____

_____

_____

_____

_____

_____

_____

NOTES

NOTES

NOTES

_____

_____

_____

_____

_____

_____

_____

_____

_____

_____

NOTES

_____

_____

_____

_____

_____

_____

_____

_____

_____

_____

_____

NOTES

_____

_____

_____

_____

_____

_____

_____

_____

_____

_____

NOTES

NOTES

_____

_____

_____

_____

_____

_____

_____

_____

_____

_____

NOTES

NOTES

NOTES

NOTES

NOTES

_____

_____

_____

_____

_____

_____

_____

_____

_____

_____

NOTES

NOTES

NOTES

NOTES

_____

_____

_____

_____

_____

_____

_____

_____

_____

_____

NOTES

NOTES

_____

_____

_____

_____

_____

_____

_____

_____

_____

_____

VEGAN RECIPES BOOK

FAVORITE VEGAN RECIPES
BOOK, APPETIZERS
ASAN SORINA

Vegan RECIPES SMOOTHIES

Vegan Smoothies: Healthy
herbal and fruit recipes
ASAN SORINA

Vegan Dessert Cookbook

Recipes for Cakes, Cookies,
Puddings, Candies, and More
ASAN SORINA

VEGAN RECIPES BOOK
MAIN-DISH

ASAN SORINA

Easy Chinese Cookbook
Healthy Chinese Cookbook for
Beginners: Simple Chinese
Recipes (Asian Food)
ASAN SORINA

My Delicious Recipes
The Ultimate Blank CookBook To
Write In Your Own Recipes |
Collect and Customize Family
Recipes In One Stylish Blank
Recipe Journal and Organizer
ASAN SORINA

The Chinese Cookbook
Fresh Recipes to Sizzle,
Steam, and Stir-Fry
Restaurant Favorites at Home,
ASAN SORINA

MY FAVORITE
RECIPES BLANK
JOURNAL
ASAN SORINA

Easy Chinese Recipes Cookbook; Restaurant Favorites Made Simple
ASAN SORINA

Easy Asian Cookbook Family-Style Favorites from East, Southeast, and South Asia
ASAN SORINA

The Ultimate Journal Chinese Recipes
ASAN SORINA

Crock-Pot Slow Cooker Recipes: Slow-Cooked Recipes to Help You Make the Most of Busy Days
ASAN SORINA

VEGAN SALDS RECIPES

Salads That Inspire: A Cookbook of Creative Salads

ASAN SORINA

Vegan Soups Recipes Book

Delicious Winter Warming Vegan Soup Recipes to Soothe Your Soul

ASAN SORINA

VEGAN SAUCES RECIPES

Easy Vegan Sauces

ASAN SORINA

DESSERT RECIPES BOOK

Quick, Easy and Delicious Recipes

ASAN SORINA

Dough and Pastries
Recipes Cookbook

ASAN SORINA

Pasta Cookbook: This Book
The Complete Recipe Book
to Cook the Most Delicious
and Tasty Dishes
ASAN SORINA

Chinese Cookbook: Easy
Recipes For Traditional
Food From China
ASAN SORINA

Easy Asian Recipes
Cookbook

ASAN SORINA

CPSIA information can be obtained
at www.ICGtesting.com
Printed in the USA
LVHW022317150621
690251LV00014B/408